THE LITTLE BOOK OF

POSITIVITY

First published in 2024 by OH
An Imprint of HEADLINE PUBLISHING GROUP

1

Disclaimer:

ISBN 978-1-03542-226-5

Compiled and written by: Jason Ward
Editorial: Saneaah Muhammad
Designed and typeset in Dosis by: Andy Jones
Project manager: Russell Porter
Production: Marion Storz
Printed and bound in China

MIX
Paper | Supporting
responsible forestry
FSC® C104740

Headline's policy is to use papers that are natural, renewable and recyclable products and made from wood grown in well-managed forests and other controlled sources. The logging and manufacturing processes are expected to conform to the environmental regulations of the country of origin.

HEADLINE PUBLISHING GROUP
An Hachette UK Company
Carmelite House, 50 Victoria Embankment, London EC4Y 0DZ

www.headline.co.uk   www.hachette.co.uk

THE LITTLE BOOK OF
POSITIVITY

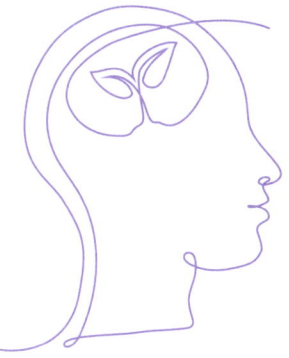

FOR WHEN LIFE
GETS A LITTLE TOUGH

CONTENTS

INTRODUCTION

Water sits in a glass. But how much water? It's a simple question, yet it has become a cliché because it challenges the possible ways in which we might view the world. A positive outlook, of course, would tell you that the glass is half full. This interpretation focuses on what is there – substance, possibility – rather than what isn't. It's an approach that's often misunderstood as naive, but this isn't the case. Positivity isn't about denying life's challenges but rather seeing the world with clear eyes and still finding the hope in it: the joy in being alive.

Hope is harder to find on some days than others. How do you remain positive when you look around you and see, well... *all this*? Turmoil, struggle, tragedy. And yet, to be positive is not blind optimism: it's choosing hope, again and again, even in the darkest moments.

Positivity is a radical act. It means cherishing the moments of promise, however slight. It means cultivating the unshakable belief that no matter what challenges come, there's always a chance to make things better.

The Little Book of Positivity is a guide to help you nurture your heart's optimism, especially when it feels elusive. Through the wisdom of inspiring minds, hopefully you'll find some motivation and resilience to carry on – to face the world head-on, yet still see its light and its beauty.

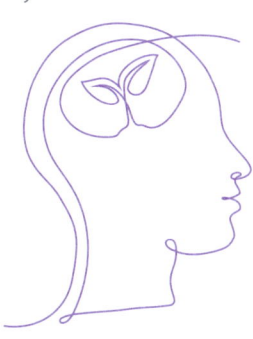

CHAPTER

1

WHEN YOU NEED INSPIRATION

Potential needs a spark to become the thing it's meant to be.

This spark isn't actually the new idea itself, whatever form that might take, but having the motivation – the *audacity* – to give it a go.

Who knows what might come from it? Who knows who you might meet?

The only joy in the world is to begin.

Cesare Pavese

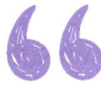

The Possible's slow fuse is lit
by the Imagination!

Emily Dickinson

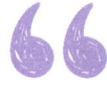

Keep your face always toward
the sunshine, and shadows
will fall behind you.

Walt Whitman

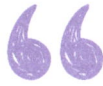

Every now and then a man's mind is
stretched by a new idea or sensation,
and never shrinks back to its former
dimensions.

Oliver Wendell Holmes Sr.

My brain takes me to places no one else lives.

Hannah Gadsby

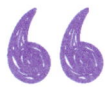

While I'm making the sushi,
I feel victorious...

Jiro Ono

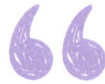

If one considered life as a simple loan,
one would perhaps be less exacting.

Eugène Delacroix

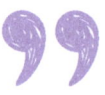

We're an impossibility in an
impossible universe.

Ray Bradbury

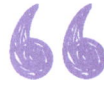

It is during our darkest moments that
we must focus to see the light.

Aristotle

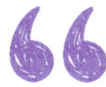

Why not you?

Steve Maraboli

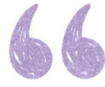

Life is too short to be little.

Benjamin Disraeli

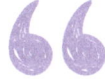

The greatest mistake you can make
in life is to be continually fearing
you will make one.

Elbert Hubbard

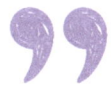

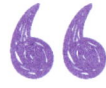

If you are curious, you will find
the puzzles around you. If you are
determined, you will solve them.

Ernő Rubik

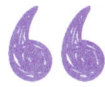

When a supremely great creative mind is kindled, it leaves a blazing trail that remains a beacon for centuries.

Subrahmanyan Chandrasekhar

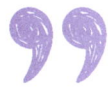

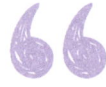

Somewhere, something incredible is waiting to be known.

Sharon Begley

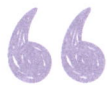

What is now proved
was once only imagined.

William Blake

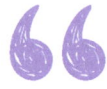

Stand before the people you
fear and speak your mind – even
if your voice shakes.

Maggie Kuhn

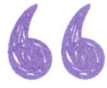

Do what you can,
with what you've got,
where you are.

Bill Widener

Because you are alive,
everything is possible.

Thich Nhat Hanh

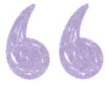

Find out what you like doing
best and get someone
to pay you for doing it.

Katharine Whitehorn

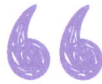

There is no cure for birth and death
save to enjoy the interval.

George Santayana

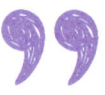

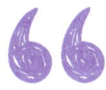

Beyond a wholesome discipline, be gentle with yourself. You are a child of the universe no less than the trees and the stars; you have a right to be here.

Max Ehrmann

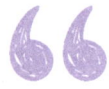

Life is the exception,
don't you forget it.

Laura Veirs

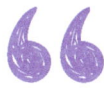

But, like ivy, we grow
where there is room for us.

Miranda July

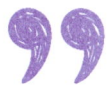

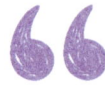

You cannot control the length
of your life, but you can control
its width and depth.

Unknown

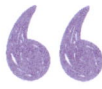

Find the good. It's all around you. Find it, showcase it and you'll start believing in it.

Jesse Owens

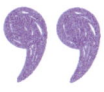

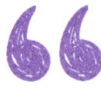

How you live your life is your business.
But remember, our hearts and our
bodies are given to us only once.

André Aciman

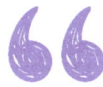

Life is very short and what we have to
do must be done in the now.

Audre Lorde

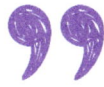

CHAPTER

2

WHEN YOU FACE ADVERSITY

Much of the time, let's be honest,
adversity is just a big thing in your way.

But adversity is not only an obstacle,
it can also be a teacher, helping you
to become the most resilient,
compassionate version of yourself.

The challenges of life test you,
but, in doing so, they also reveal your
strengths.

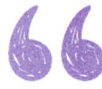

You might encounter many defeats, but you must never be defeated.

Maya Angelou

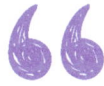

Rain does not deter them,
nor does darkness.

"Highland Midge" Wikipedia entry

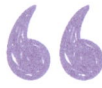

It is often the failure who is the pioneer
in new lands, new undertakings,
and new forms of expression.

Eric Hoffer

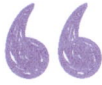

A problem is a chance for you
to do your best.

Duke Ellington

One day in retrospect, the years of
struggle will strike you as
the most beautiful.

Sigmund Freud

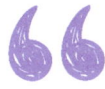

Optimism is a happiness magnet. If
you stay positive, good things and good
people will be drawn to you.

Mary Lou Retton

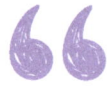

A ship in harbour is safe,
but that is not what ships are for.

John Augustus Shedd

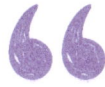

We are not interested in the possibilities
of defeat; they do not exist.

Queen Victoria

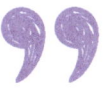

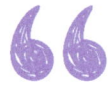

No matter how far away from yourself you may have strayed, there is always a path back. You already know who you are and how to fulfill your destiny.

Oprah Winfrey

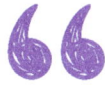

No matter what situation you're in,
find something good about it.

Cherokee proverb

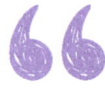

Vitality shows not only in the ability to persist but in the ability to start over.

F. Scott Fitzgerald

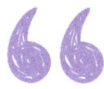

You, me, or nobody is gonna hit as hard as life. But it ain't about how hard you hit. It's about how hard you can get hit and keep moving forward.

Sylvester Stallone

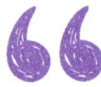

In the middle of difficulty lies
opportunity.

John Archibald Wheeler

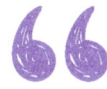

If they don't give you a seat at the table,
bring in a folding chair.

Shirley Chisholm

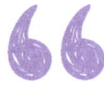

Not everything that is faced
can be changed; but nothing can
be changed until it is faced.

James Baldwin

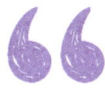

He did not hate the Winter now,
for he knew that it was merely
the Spring asleep.

Oscar Wilde

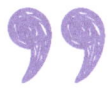

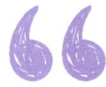

Your heart's not broken,
it's only growing.

Rich Rinaldi

In three words I can sum up everything
I've learned about life. It goes on.

Robert Frost

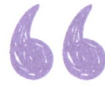

What is defeat? Nothing but education – nothing but the first step to something better.

Wendell Phillips

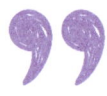

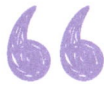

I keep on making what
I can't do yet in order to learn
to be able to do it.

Vincent Van Gogh

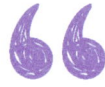

A certain amount of opposition is a great help to a man. Kites rise against not with the wind. Even a head wind is better than nothing.

John Neal

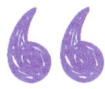

He who is not courageous enough
to take risks will accomplish
nothing in life.

Muhammad Ali

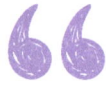

We are never so happy
or so unhappy as we suppose.

François de La Rochefoucauld

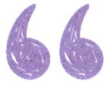

Visits always give pleasure –
if not the arrival, the departure.

Portuguese proverb

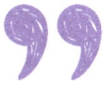

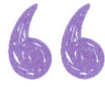

In the middle of winter I at last discovered that there was in me an invincible summer.

Albert Camus

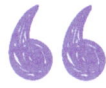

Ain't no shame in holding on to grief,
as long as you make room for
other things too.

George Pelecanos

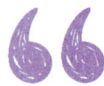

Water is patient. Dripping water wears away a stone. Remember that, my child. Remember you are half water. If you can't go through an obstacle, go around it. Water does.

Margaret Atwood

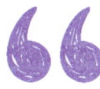

I am a pear that has survived a hailstorm: when it does not rot, it becomes better and sweeter than the others, in spite of its little scars.

Colette

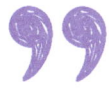

CHAPTER

3

WHEN DOUBT CREEPS IN

Caution can be valuable – it's helpful when you fancy climbing into an old fridge at a landfill – but so often it clouds your judgement.

More often than not, self-doubt is like you've invited your biggest, most critical enemy to live in your head.

Caution would advise against doing that, too.

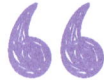

One bright day
none of this will matter.

Rose Elinor Dougall

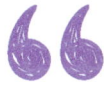

Everything works out in the end.
If it didn't, it's because it hasn't
come to an end yet.

Domingos Sabino

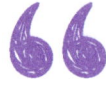

When something's not right, it's wrong.

Bob Dylan

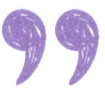

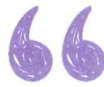

Doubt is an uncomfortable condition,
but certainty is a ridiculous one.

Voltaire

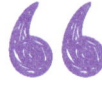

Don't take life so serious son ... it ain't nohow permanent.

Walt Kelly

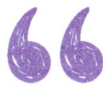

Hope is generally a wrong guide,
though it is very good company
by the way.

George Savile, 1st Marquess of Halifax

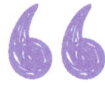

In order to go on living one must try to escape the death involved in perfection.

Hannah Arendt

You wouldn't worry so much about what others think of you if you realized how seldom they do.

Eleanor Roosevelt

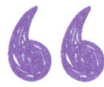

A life spent in making mistakes is not only more honourable but more useful than a life spent doing nothing.

George Bernard Shaw

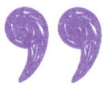

When in doubt, doubt the doubt!

Deepak Chopra

The willingness to accept responsibility
for one's own life is the source from
which self-respect springs.

Joan Didion

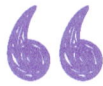

Get used to the bear behind you.

Werner Herzog

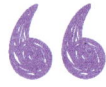

Were the diver to think on the jaws of the shark, he would never lay hands on the precious pearl.

Saadi

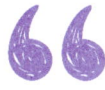

When you hear about something terrible, calm yourself by asking, 'If there had been an equally positive improvement, would I have heard about that?'

Hans Rosling

It makes absolutely no difference what people think of you.

Rumi

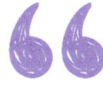

We look into mirrors but we only see
the effects of our times on us – not our
effect on others.

Pearl Bailey

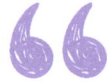

We succeed in enterprises which demand the positive qualities we possess, but we excel in those which can also make use of our defects.

Alexis de Tocqueville

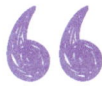

Only those who will risk going too
far can possibly find out how far
one can go.

T. S. Eliot

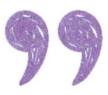

We must be willing to get rid of the life we've planned, so as to have the life that is waiting for us.

Joseph Campbell

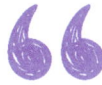

Change your life today. Don't gamble on the future, act now, without delay.

Simone de Beauvoir

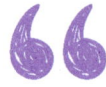

Too much success is not an advantage.
Do not tinkle like jade.
Or clatter like stone chimes.

Lao Tzu

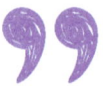

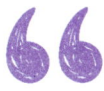

Each time you fail, start all over again, and you will grow stronger until you find that you have accomplished a purpose – not the one you began with, perhaps, but one that you will be glad to remember.

Anne Sullivan

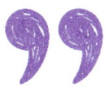

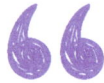

Our doubts are traitors
And make us lose the good we
oft might win
By fearing to attempt.

William Shakespeare

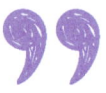

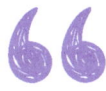

For the truth, it is ever the fitting
time; who wait until circumstances
completely favour his undertaking, will
never accomplish anything, but will
remain in inactivity.

Johann Eduard Huther

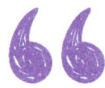

You can either waltz boldly on to the stage of life and live the way you know your spirit is nudging you to, or you can sit quietly by the wall, receding into the shadows of fear and self doubt.

Oprah Winfrey

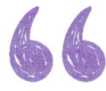

You won't get younger than you're feeling now.

Mirah Yom Tov Zeitlyn

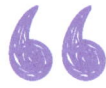

If it can't go on forever it will stop.

Herbert Stein

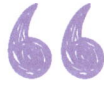

It was the possibility of darkness that made the day seem so bright.

Stephen King

CHAPTER

4

WHEN YOU SEEK JOY

It's normal to forget this, but so much of life is inherently joyful – even the mundane bits are miraculous when viewed in the right light.

We're not here for very long and sometimes, just scrunching up your toes on a good carpet is enough to make you feel lucky to be alive.

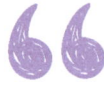

You will find poetry nowhere unless you bring some of it with you.

Joseph Joubert

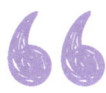

How crisp, how bright a world!

Nan Shepherd

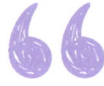

Every day above ground is a great day.

Pitbull

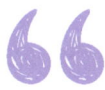

I, too, have my religion. It is this:
Happiness is the only good. The time to
be happy is now; the place to be happy
is here; and the way to be happy is to
make others happy. This is the religion
of usefulness; this is the religion
of reason.

Robert G. Ingersoll

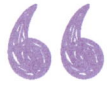

Find the good and praise it, speak
sparingly of the bad.

Madison Babcock

The best is yet to come.

Frank Sinatra

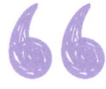

I always prefer to believe
the best of everybody.
It saves so much trouble.

Rudyard Kipling

When a man loves cats,
I am his friend and comrade,
without further introduction.

Mark Twain

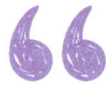

Breathe in the pine and mint from the little salt marsh; its fragrance is scratching at the gate like a cat!

Colette

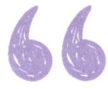

I think of beauty as an absolute necessity. I don't think it's a privilege or an indulgence, it's not even a quest. I think it's almost like knowledge, which is to say, it's what we were born for.

Toni Morrison

You just can't compete
with the way green treetops
look against a blue sky.

Amy Krouse Rosenthal

Nothing which makes us
happy is an illusion.

Johann Wolfgang von Goethe

I looked down at my shoes.
I wasn't in a hurry. I never have to
be any particular place at any particular
time. Let time watch me, not me it.

Olga Tokarczuk

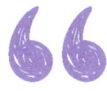

It's a lovely feeling to almost be lost, but not quite, and to feel you are being led down mysterious paths.

Kate Humble

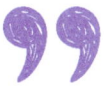

In the vastness of space and the
immensity of time, it is my joy
to share a planet.

Carl Sagan

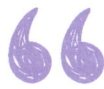

There may be peace without joy,
and joy without peace, but the two
combined make happiness.

John Buchan

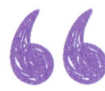

Happy are those who sing
with all their heart, in the
forthrightness of their heart.
Find joy in the sky, in the trees,
in the flowers. There are flowers
everywhere for those who
want to see them.

Henri Matisse

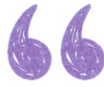

Observe the wonders as they
occur around you. Don't claim them.
Feel the artistry moving through,
and be silent.

Rumi

I have learned,
When things are beautiful ,
To just keep on.

Bill Callahan

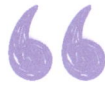

Through love, through friendship,
a heart lives more than one life and
is made joyful or sorrowful by the
experiences of many others.

Anaïs Nin

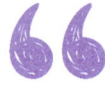

I just wish the world was twice as big –
and half of it was still unexplored.

David Attenborough

Joy does not come from what you do,
it flows into what you do and thus into
this world from deep within you.

Eckhart Tolle

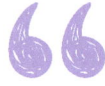

Smile, breathe and go slowly.

Thich Nhat Hanh

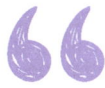

When the spirits are low, when the day appears dark, when work becomes monotonous, when hopes seem hardly worth having, just mount a bicycle and go for a good spin down the road, without thought of anything but the ride you are taking.

Sir Arthur Conan Doyle

If the sight of the blue skies fills you with joy, if a blade of grass springing up in the fields has power to move you, rejoice, for your soul is alive.

Eleonora Duse

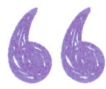

There are those who give with joy, and
that joy is their reward.

Kahlil Gibran

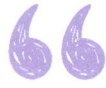

Find ecstasy in life; the mere sense of living is joy enough.

Emily Dickinson

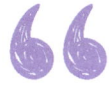

But for now we are young,
Let us lay in the sun,
And count every beautiful,
thing we can see.

Jeff Mangum

CHAPTER

5

WHEN YOU LONG FOR CHANGE

Why would anyone want to leave their comfort zone? It's comfortable, that's the whole point.

And yet, embracing change can bring growth, renewal, a new perspective.

Maybe a better way to look at it is that you're not leaving your comfort zone, but instead charting your own course – boldly, rakishly – towards a new, better one.

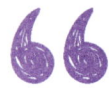

Most people overestimate what they can do in a day, and underestimate what they can do in a month. We overestimate what we can do in a year, and underestimate what we can accomplish in a decade.

Matthew Kelly

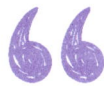

When I dare to be powerful, to use
my strength in the service of my
vision, then it becomes less important
whether or not I am unafraid.

Audre Lorde

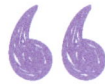

Regret for the things we did can be
tempered by time; it is regret for the
things we did not do that
is inconsolable.

Sydney J. Harris

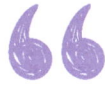

You can't turn back the clock. But
you can wind it up again.

Bonnie Prudden

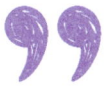

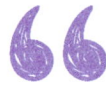

Look at the blue of the sky and tell me why you held back. Did you think there would one day be a bluer sky and a better hour?

Morrissey

What do we live for,
if it is not to make life less
difficult for each other?

George Eliot

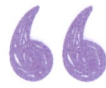

You can't cross the sea merely by standing and staring at the water.

Rabindranath Tagore

It's not that we have a short time to live, but that we waste much of it. Life is long enough, and it's been given to us in generous measure for accomplishing the greatest things, if the whole of it is well invested.

Seneca the Younger

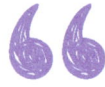

Do things and feel happiness.

Pete Holmes

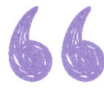

When given the chance, always swim in the waterfall, no matter how slippery the climb down.

Unknown

The greatest discovery of all time is that a person can change his future by merely changing his attitude.

Oprah Winfrey

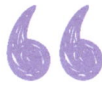

The only way to make sense out of change is to plunge into it, move with it and join the dance.

Alan Watts

We turn not older with years,
but newer every day.

Emily Dickinson

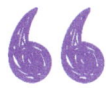

The afternoon of life is just as full of meaning as the morning; only, its meaning and purpose are different.

Carl Jung

It is far better to light the candle
than to curse the darkness.

William L. Watkinson

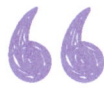

Change will not come if we wait for some other person or some other time. We are the ones we've been waiting for. We are the change that we seek.

Barack Obama

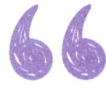

Until you dig a hole, you plant a tree,
you water it and make it survive,
you haven't done a thing.
You are just talking.

Wangarī Maathai

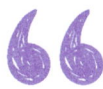

I'm not waiting for anything.
I'm trying to make it all happen. I wish
I hadn't waited for a lot of things.
If you want to hear from the old guy:
don't put off joy.

William H. Macy

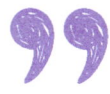

The mystery of human existence lies not in just staying alive, but in finding something to live for.

Fyodor Dostoevsky

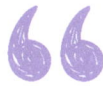

Nothing will ever just come to you,
it's only what you find around
and what you do.

Matt Berninger

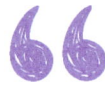

Every passing minute is another chance
to turn it all around.

Cameron Crowe

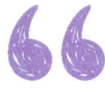

I try to be as philosophical as the old lady who said that the best thing about the future is that it only comes one day at a time.

Dean Acheson

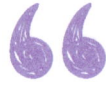

Don't waste your time on jealousy. Sometimes you're ahead, sometimes you're behind. The race is long and, in the end, it's only with yourself.

Mary Schmich

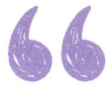

No wise man ever wished
to be younger.

Jonathan Swift

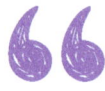

Yesterday is dead, tomorrow hasn't arrived yet. I have just one day, today, and I'm going to be happy in it.

Groucho Marx

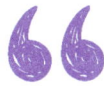

There are far better things ahead than
any we leave behind.

C. S. Lewis

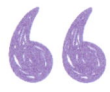

If you always do what you've always done, you always get what you've always gotten.

Jessie Potter

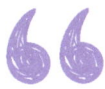

Why not go out on a limb?
Isn't that where the fruit is?

Frank Scully

CHAPTER
6

WHEN YOU NEED RESILIENCE

It's easy to be upbeat, graceful and magnanimous when everything is going well.

The most truly positive action you can take in life is getting back up again after you've been knocked down.

That inner fortitude is fundamentally optimistic: it's a hope that you can endure, a hope that – as in nature – today will end, and tomorrow will come.

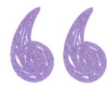

Resistance is first of all a matter
of principle and a way to live, to
make yourself one small republic of
unconquered spirit.

Rebecca Solnit

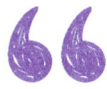

Optimism is a weapon.

Josie Long

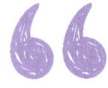

Hope is the feeling we have that the feeling we have is not permanent.

Mignon McLaughlin

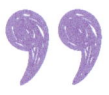

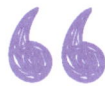

Finish every day, and be done with it.

Ralph Waldo Emerson

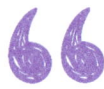

Most of the important things in the world have been accomplished by people who have kept on trying when there seemed to be no hope at all.

Dale Carnegie

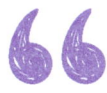

Life is either a daring adventure
or nothing. To keep our faces toward
change and behave like free spirits
in the presence of fate is strength
undefeatable.

Helen Keller

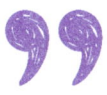

Life is bristling with thorns,
and I know no other remedy than
to cultivate one's garden.

Voltaire

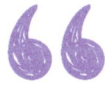

I still believe that peace and plenty
and happiness can be worked out some
way. I am a fool.

Kurt Vonnegut

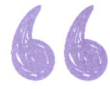

A certain class of people are fond of talking about 'the good old days', but they are for the most part individuals without imagination and with a very poor memory.

H. B. Meyers

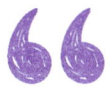

It is really wonderful how much resilience there is in human nature. Let any obstructing cause, no matter what, be removed in any way, even by death, and we fly back to first principles of hope and enjoyment.

Bram Stoker

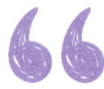

Rest satisfied with doing well, and leave others to talk of you as they please.

Pythagoras

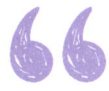

We all have moments of anxiety
or stress or confusion or sadness.
Sometimes it can be really hard to
articulate that to another person. You
can talk to a tree: they feel old and wise
and at times you need an old and wise
thing that isn't going to judge you.

Kate Humble

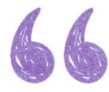

Don't be afraid to be confused. Try to remain permanently confused. Anything is possible. Stay open, forever, so open it hurts, and then open up some more, until the day you die, world without end.

George Saunders

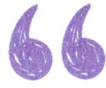

Do not judge me by my success, judge me by how many times I fell down and got back up again.

Nelson Mandela

What you risk reveals what you value.

Jeanette Winterson

I believe any success in life is made by going into an area with a blind, furious optimism.

Sylvester Stallone

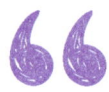

It seems to me that the natural world is the greatest source of excitement; the greatest source of visual beauty; the greatest source of intellectual interest. It is the greatest source of so much in life that makes life worth living.

David Attenborough

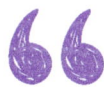

March on. Do not tarry.
To go forward is to move toward
perfection. March on, and fear not
the thorns, or the sharp stones
on life's path.

Kahlil Gibran

Life always has an unhappy ending,
but you can have a lot of fun along the
way, and everything doesn't have to be
dripping in deep significance.

Roger Ebert

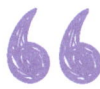

Every day is the prime of your life.

Amy Krouse Rosenthal

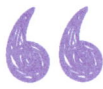

Courage doesn't always roar.
Sometimes courage is a quiet voice
at the end of the day saying, 'I will try
again tomorrow.'

Mary Anne Radmacher

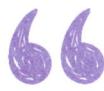

You can't go back and make a new
start, but you can start right now and
make a brand new ending.

James R. Sherman

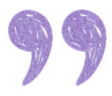

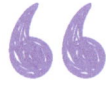

The world breaks everyone and afterward many are strong at the broken places.

Ernest Hemingway

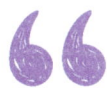

I thought all the bad stuff would go away, but actually it all came rushing back and dominated my thoughts. And I realised I had to take it all on directly. That kind of past is like a big rucksack full of bricks. You can lug it around all your life if you like. Or you can find a way to put it down and walk away.

Billy Connolly

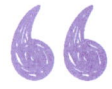

I shall never have the garden I have in my mind, but that for me is the joy of it; certain things can never be realized and so all the more reason to attempt them. A garden, no matter how good it is, must never completely satisfy.

Jamaica Kincaid

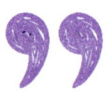

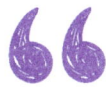

Things usually make sense in time,
and even bad decisions have their own
kind of correctness.

Miranda July

This is my time and I am
thrilled to be alive.

Michael Stipe

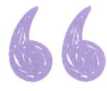

Nana korobi, ya oki.
(Fall seven times, stand up eight.)

Japanese proverb

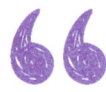

Every end in history necessarily
contains a new beginning.

Hannah Arendt

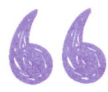

What we have once enjoyed we can never lose. A sunset, a mountain bathed in moonlight, the ocean in calm and in storm – we see these, love their beauty, hold the vision to our hearts. All that we love deeply becomes a part of us.

Helen Keller

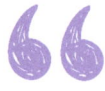

With all its sham, drudgery, and broken
dreams, it is still a beautiful world.

Max Ehrmann

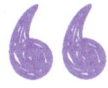

I understand and I wish to continue.

Legal disclaimer, the internet

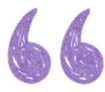

We cannot cure the world of sorrows,
but we can choose to live in joy.

Joseph Campbell

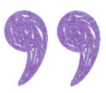